Famous & Fun Christmas Duets

6 Duets for One Piano, Four Hands

Carol Matz

Famous & Fun Christmas Duets, Book 4, contains 6 carefully selected Christmas favorites. The duets are arranged in equal parts for early intermediate pianists, and are written for one piano, four hands. For easier reading, each part is written using both treble and bass clefs, with directions for the *primo* to play up an octave and the *secondo* down an octave. Additionally, the melody often shifts between *primo* and *secondo*, creating interesting parts for both players. Book 4 features arrangements in the keys of F and D major, as well as A minor and E minor. Students are sure to enjoy their experience with these fun duets!

Carol Matz

Alfred Music
P.O. Box 10003
Van Nuys, CA 91410-0003
alfred.com

ISBN-10: 1-4706-1726-9
ISBN-13: 978-1-4706-1726-4

Angels We Have Heard On High

Secondo

Traditional
Arranged by Carol Matz

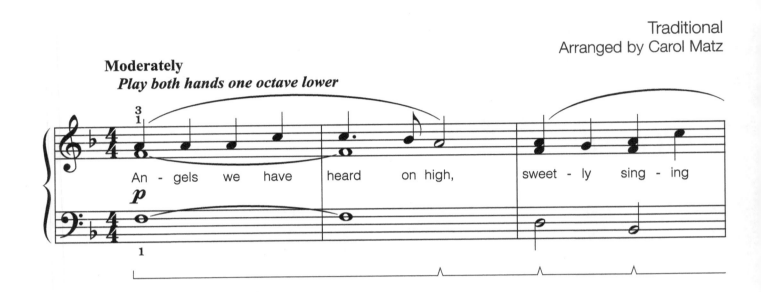

Angels We Have Heard On High

Primo

Traditional
Arranged by Carol Matz

Moderately
Play both hands one octave higher

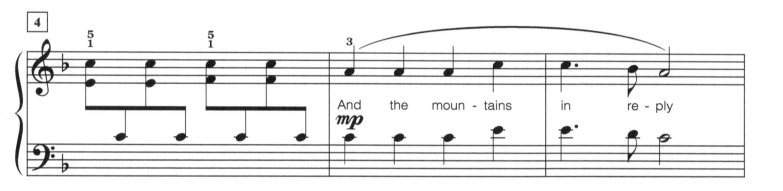

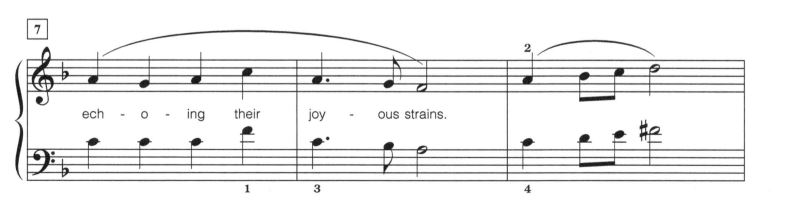

4

Secondo

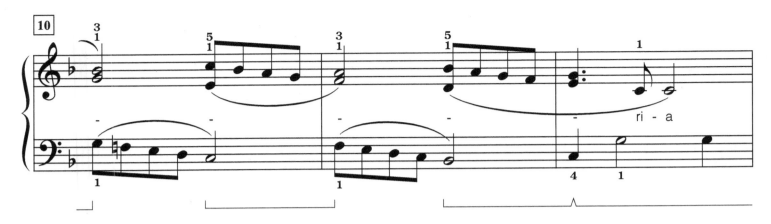

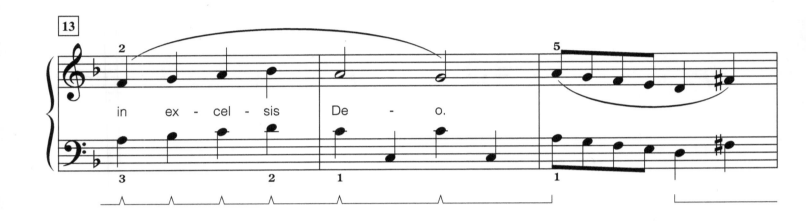

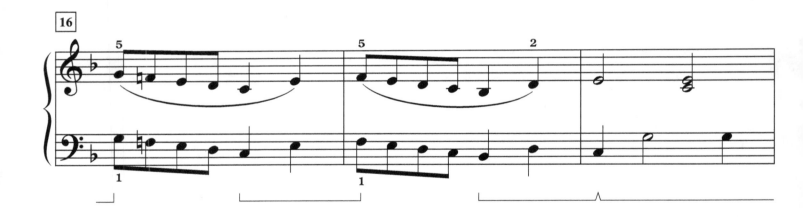

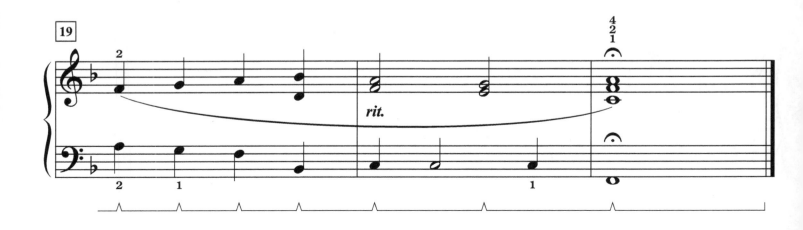

Primo

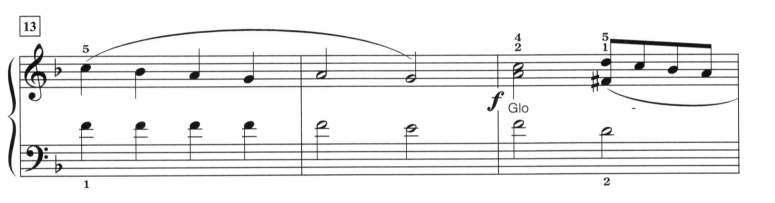

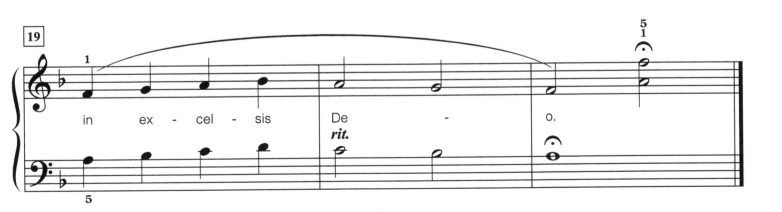

We Three Kings of Orient Are

Secondo

John Henry Hopkins, Jr.
Arranged by Carol Matz

We Three Kings of Orient Are

Primo

John Henry Hopkins, Jr.
Arranged by Carol Matz

Flowing
Play both hands one octave higher

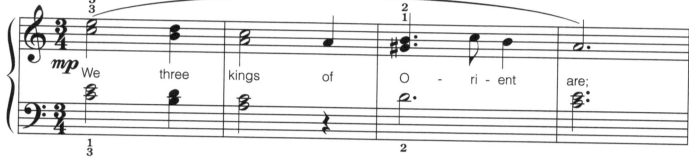

We three kings of O - ri - ent are;

bear - ing gifts we trav - erse a - far.

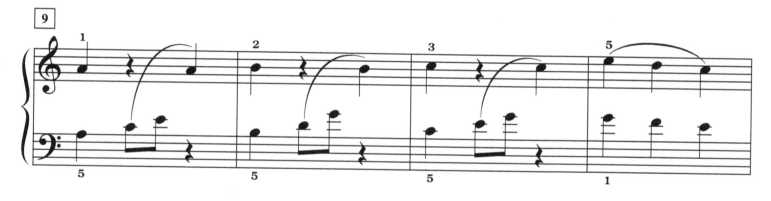

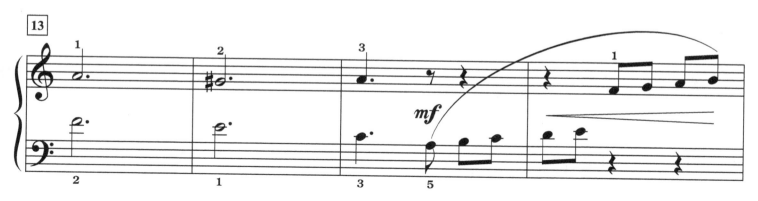

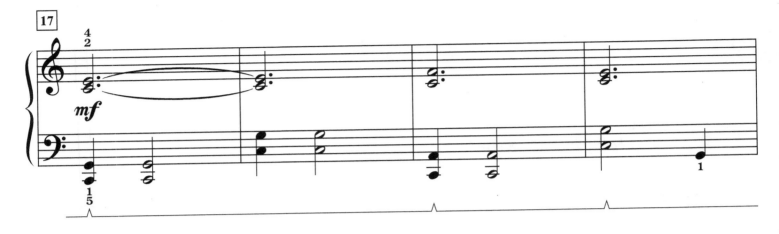

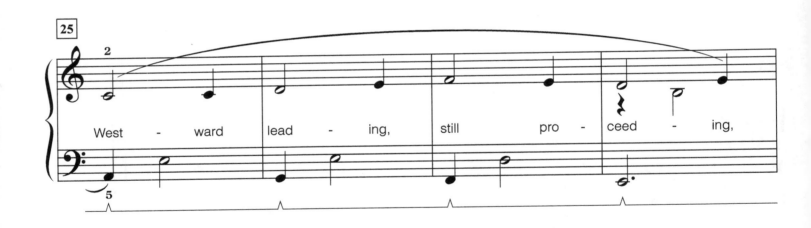

West - ward lead - ing, still pro - ceed - ing,

Primo

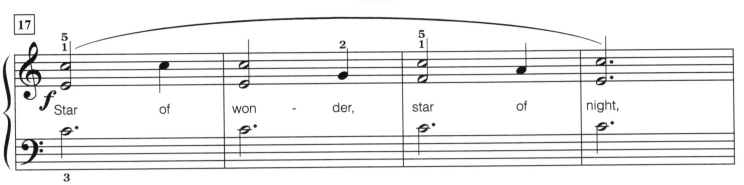

Star of won - der, star of night,

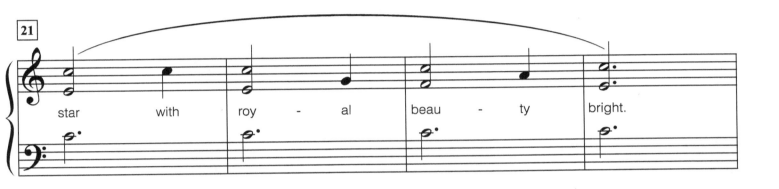

star with roy - al beau - ty bright.

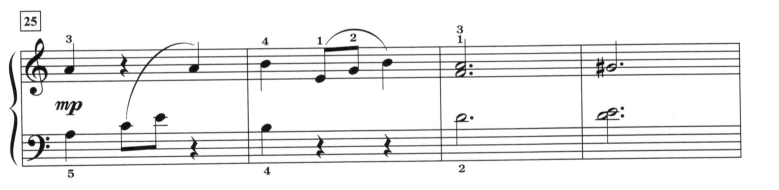

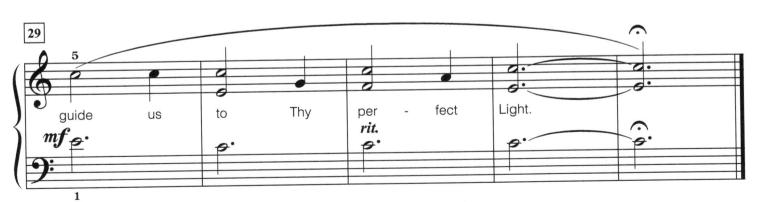

guide us to Thy per - fect Light.

What Child Is This?

Secondo

Words by William C. Dix
Traditional English Melody
Arranged by Carol Matz

What Child Is This?

Primo

Words by William C. Dix
Traditional English Melody
Arranged by Carol Matz

Moderately

Play both hands one octave higher

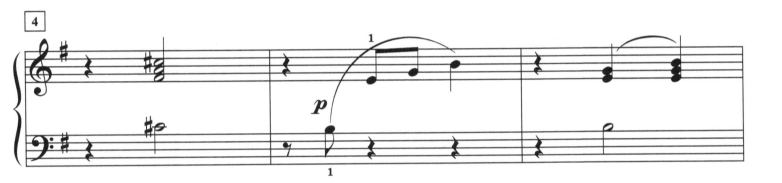

whom

Secondo

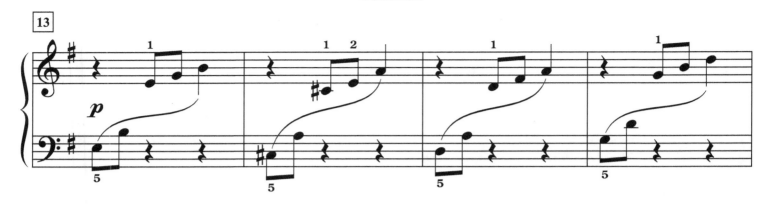

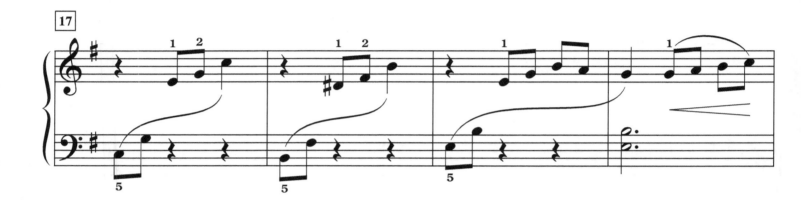

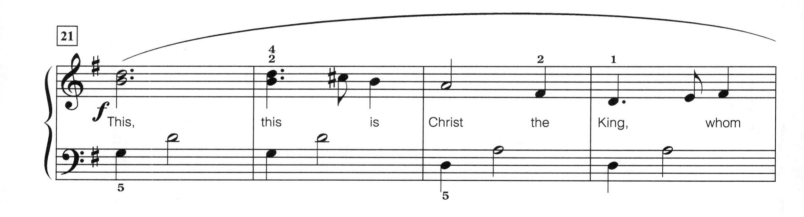

This, this is Christ the King, whom

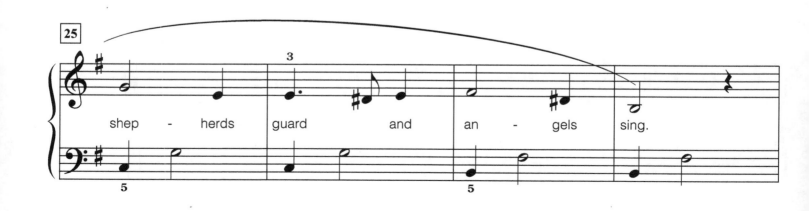

shep - herds guard and an - gels sing.

Primo

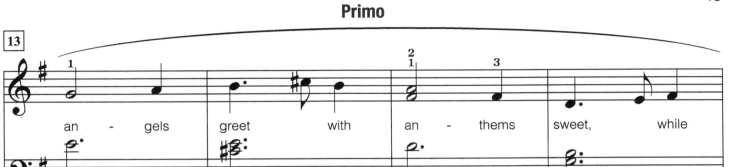

an - gels greet with an - thems sweet, while

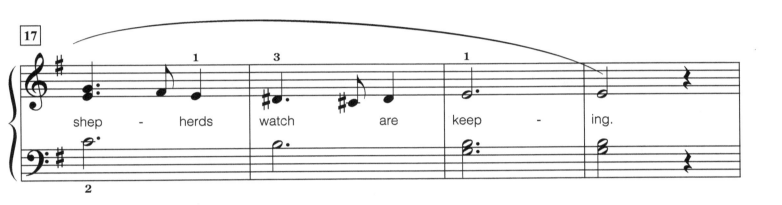

shep - herds watch are keep - ing.

Secondo

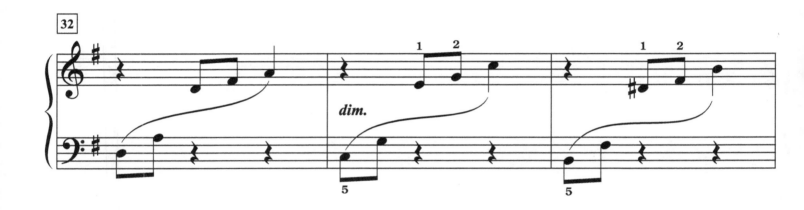

Primo

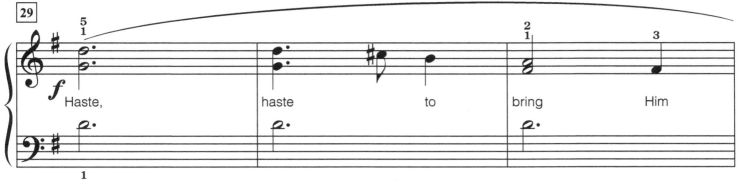

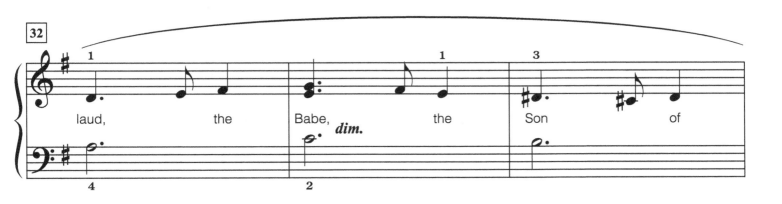

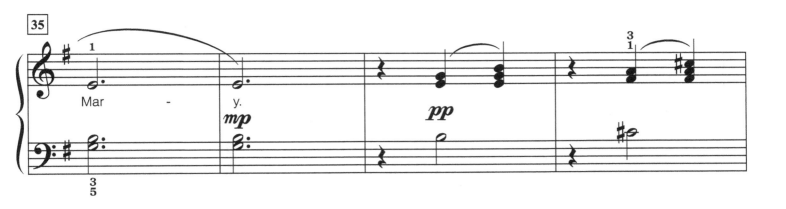

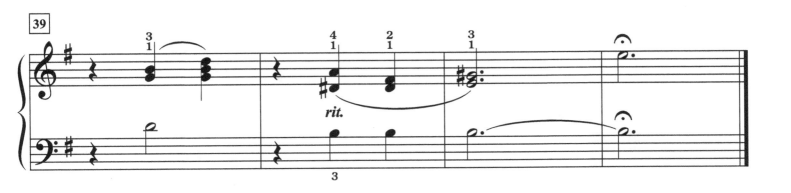

The First Noel

Secondo

Traditional English Carol
Arranged by Carol Matz

Flowing
Play both hands one octave lower

The first No - el, the an - gel did say, was to cer - tain poor shep - herds in fields as they lay.

The First Noel

Primo

Traditional English Carol
Arranged by Carol Matz

Flowing
Play both hands one octave higher

Secondo

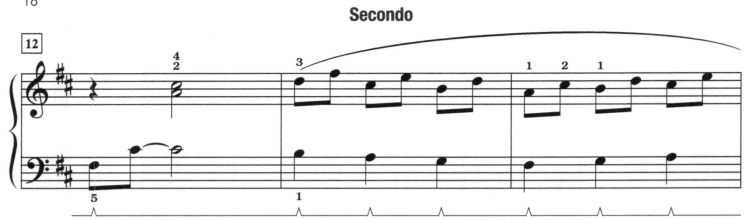

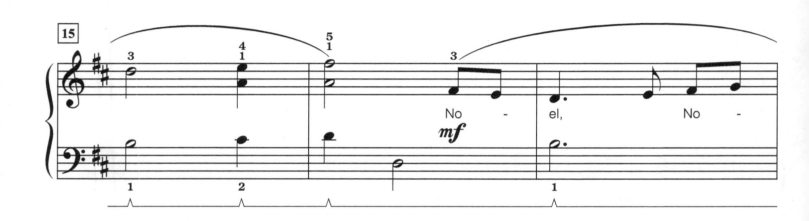

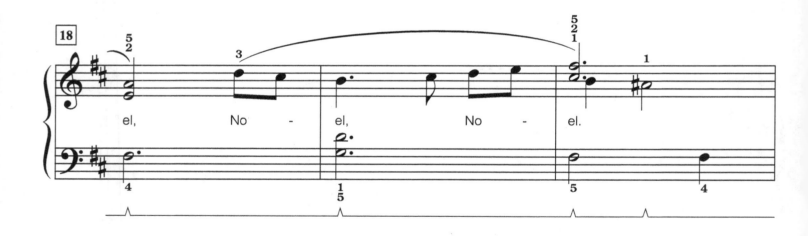

Primo

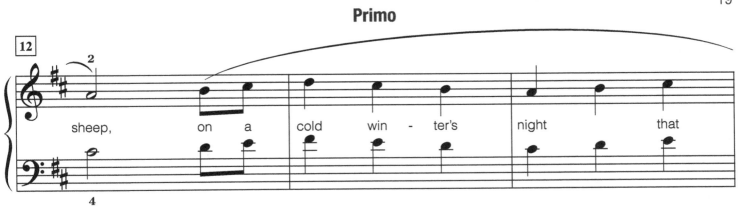

sheep,   on a   cold win - ter's   night   that

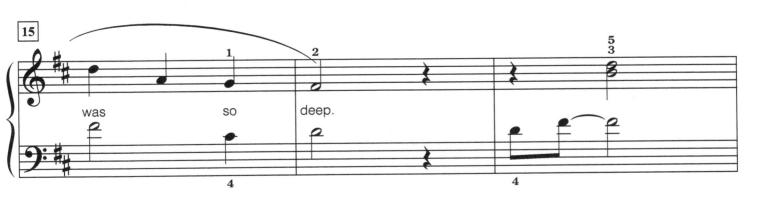

was   so   deep.

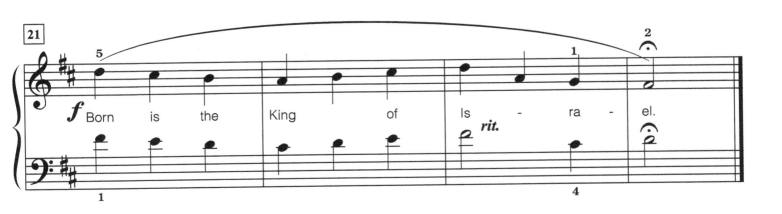

f Born is the   King   of   Is - ra - el.   *rit.*

Bring a Torch, Jeannette, Isabella

Secondo

Traditional French Carol
Arranged by Carol Matz

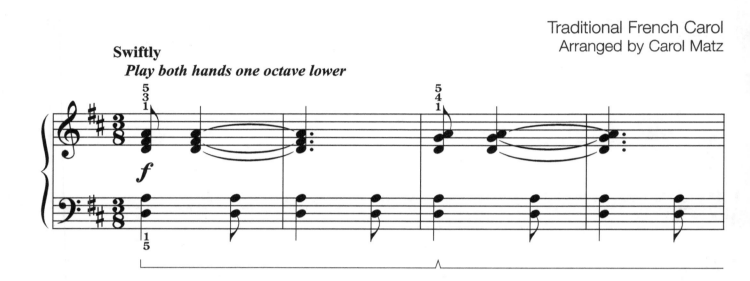

Bring a Torch, Jeannette, Isabella

Primo

Traditional French Carol
Arranged by Carol Matz

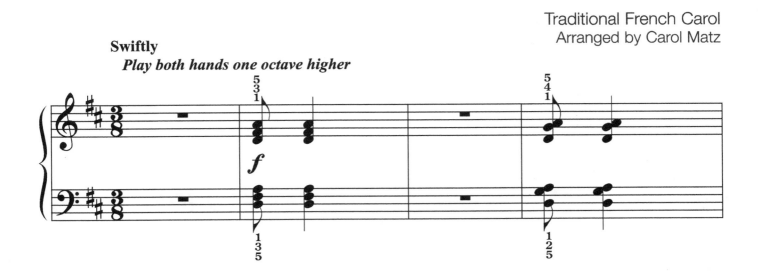

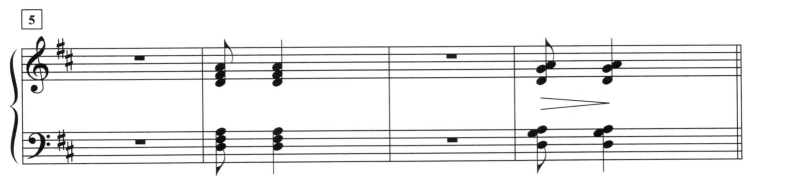

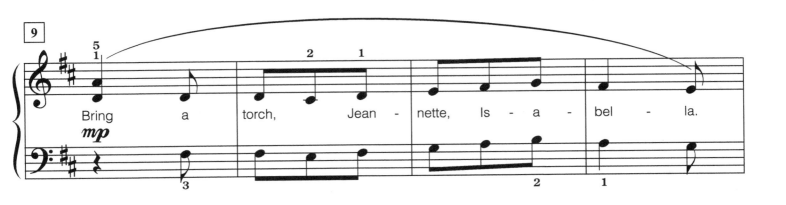

Secondo

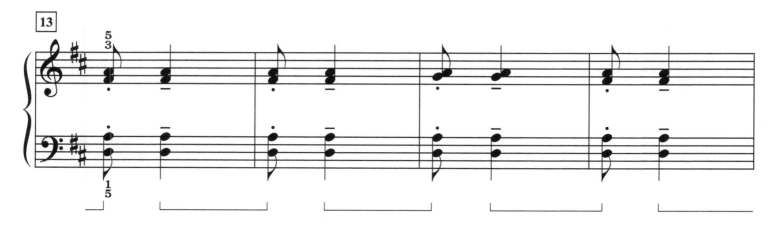

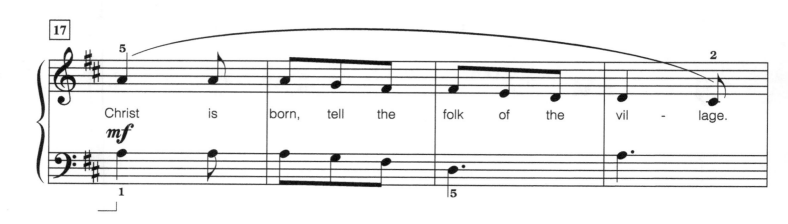

Christ is born, tell the folk of the vil - lage.

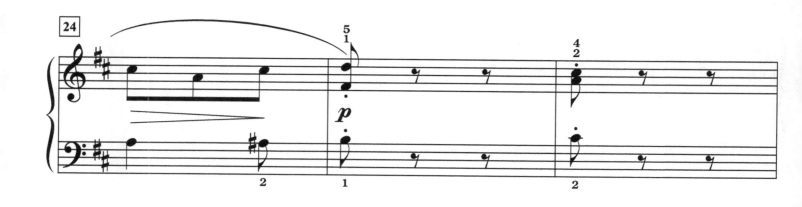

Primo

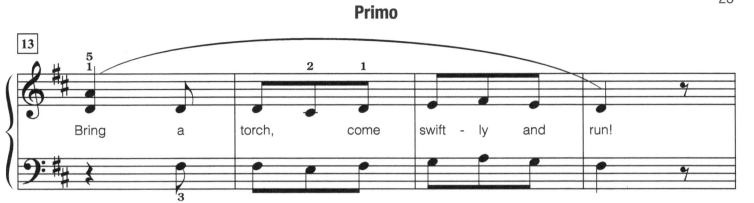

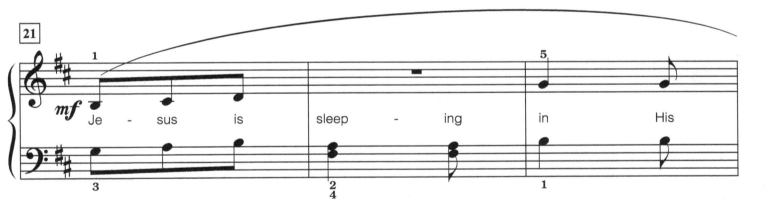

Secondo

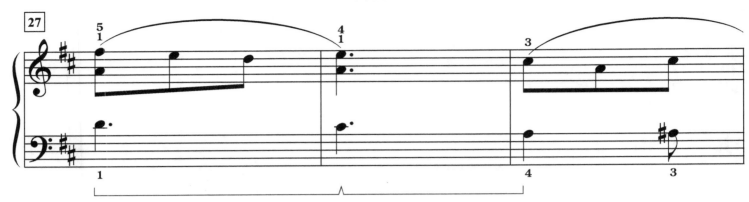

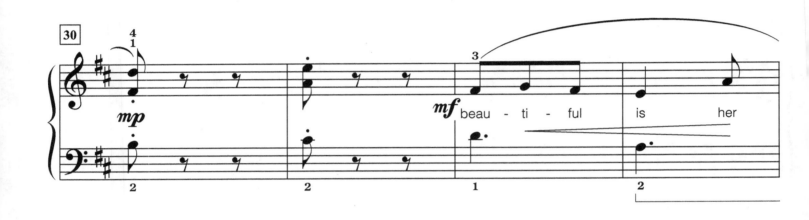

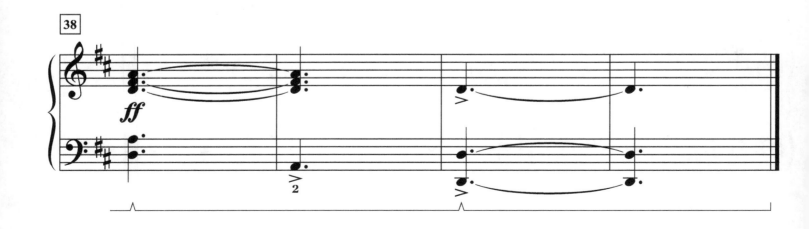

Primo

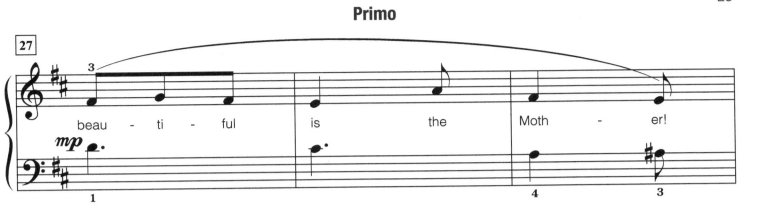

beau - ti - ful is the Moth - er!

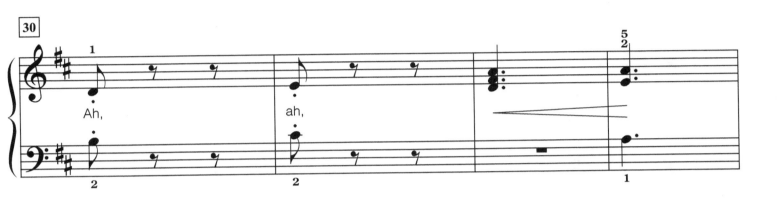

Ah, ah,

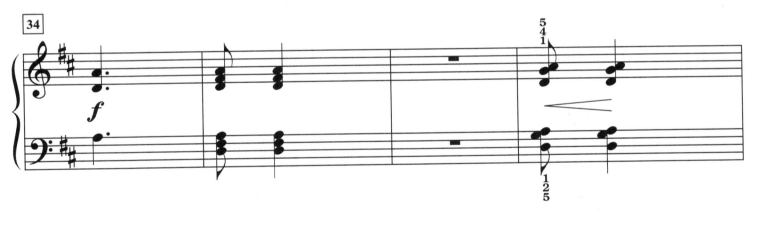

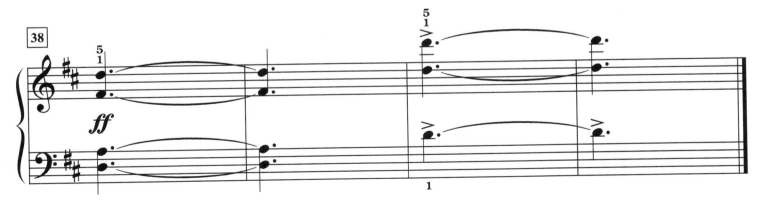

The Hallelujah Chorus

(from *Messiah*)

Secondo

George Frideric Handel
Arranged by Carol Matz

Moderately fast

Play both hands one octave lower

The Hallelujah Chorus

(from *Messiah*)

Primo

George Frideric Handel
Arranged by Carol Matz

Secondo

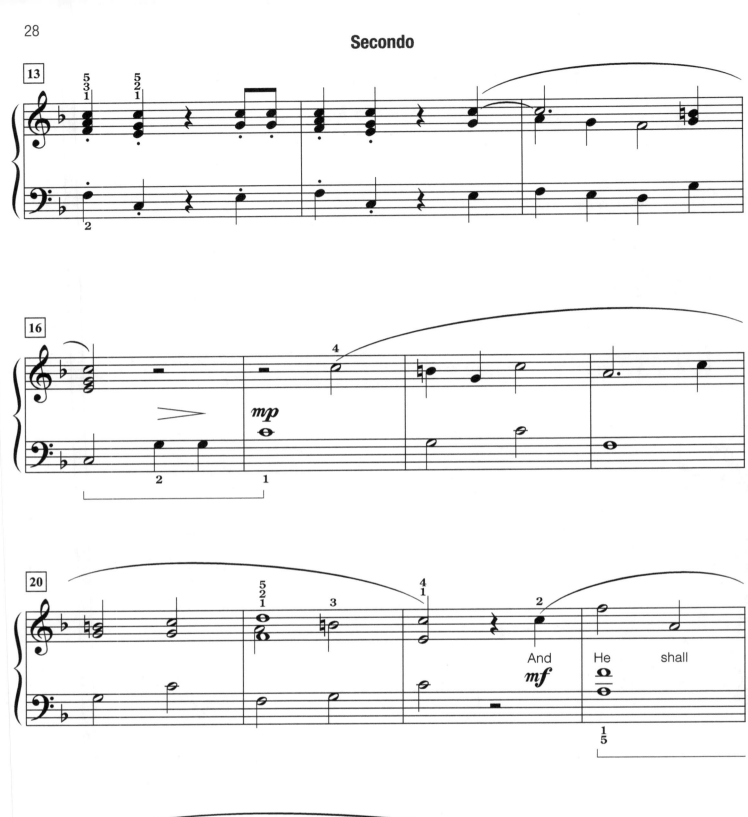

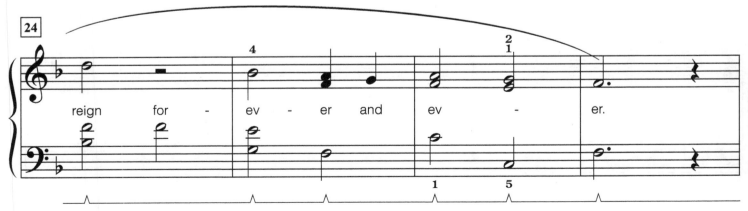

Primo

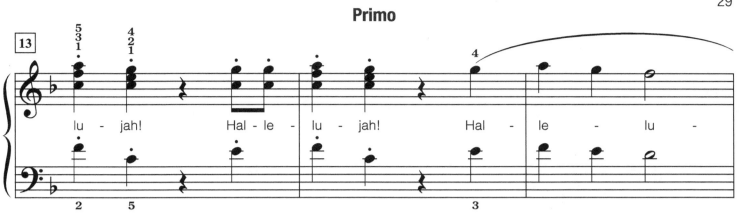

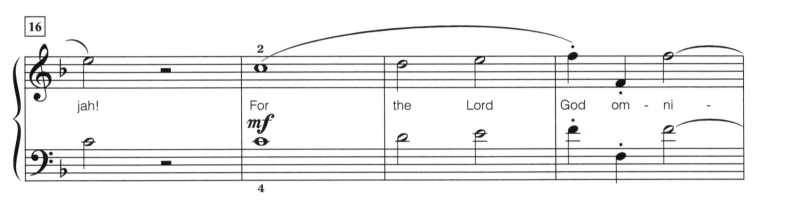

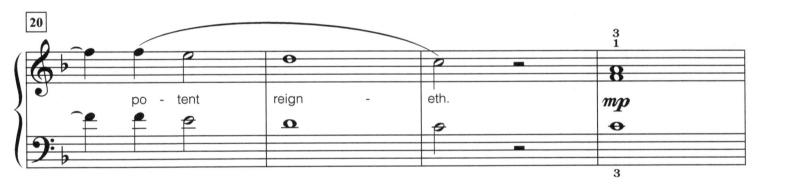

Secondo

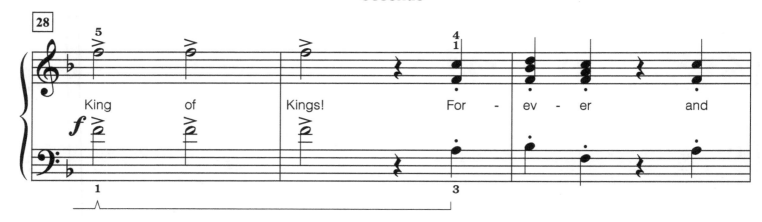

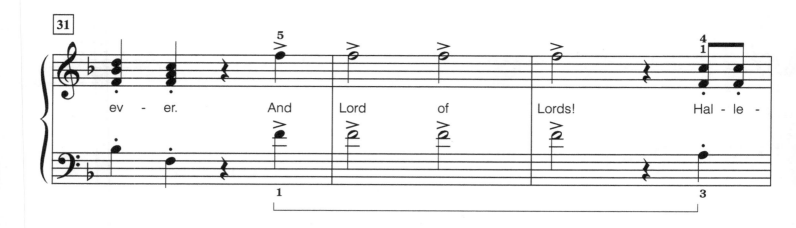

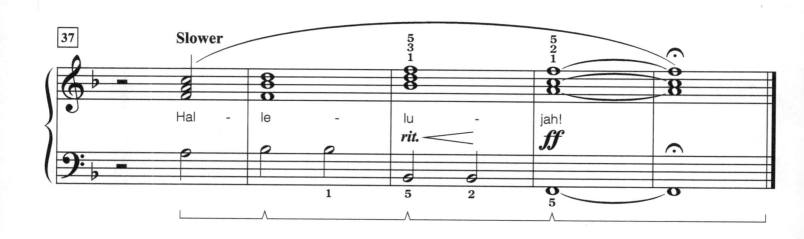

Primo

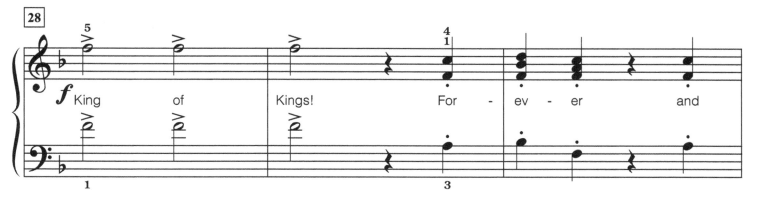

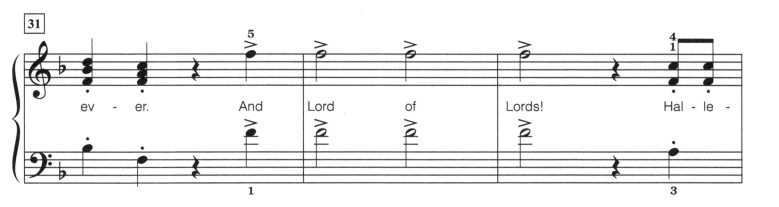

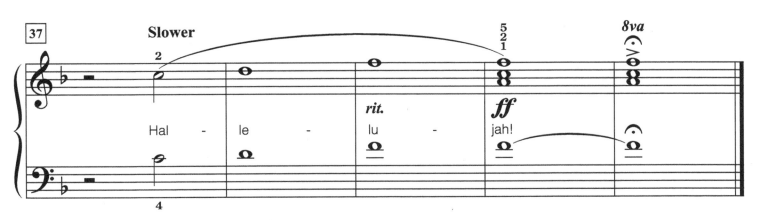